790
RF

M000249283

The Heinemann First Encyclopedia

Index

Heinemann Library
Des Plaines, Illinois

Contents

AMERICAN HISTORY

Early America 4

The First Settlers 6

The Revolutionary War 8

Civil War 10

America Grows 12

The World at War 14

The 1950s and 1960s.. 16

THE INDEX

How to Use This Index 17

The Subject List 18

Index.. 23

EARLY AMERICA

About 30 thousand years ago, the Bering Land Bridge connected Asia to North America. Asian hunters followed animals into North America. They did not know they were going to a new continent where people had not lived before.

This painting of a Native American village was made in the 1500s.

Native Americans

Those hunters are the ancestors of Native Americans. They hunted mammoths, giant bison, deer, and elk. They lived in deserts, forests, mountains, and on the great plains. When Columbus came, two thousand Native American tribes lived in America. Eight million Native Americans lived north of what is now Mexico.

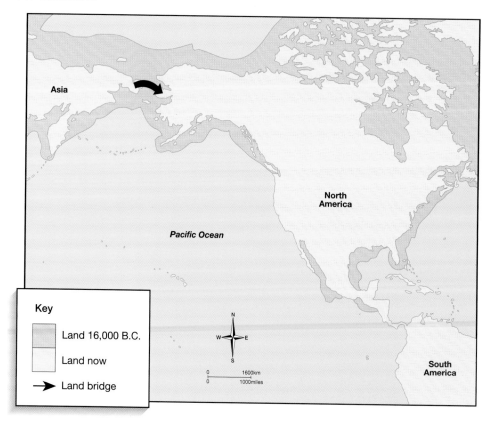

Christopher Columbus

In 1492, Christopher Columbus sailed west across the Atlantic Ocean. He was looking for spices and gold in Asia. Instead, he landed on an island several hundred miles off the coast of what is now Florida. He died in 1506, never knowing he had reached America.

Early Explorers

Other European explorers followed Columbus to America. They looked for gold, slaves, land, and spices. By 1513, they knew the Americas were two continents.

Columbus claimed the islands he landed on for Spain.

Date	Explorer	Country	Area Explored
1492	Christopher Columbus	Spain	Caribbean, South America
1497	John Cabot	England	Northeast North America
1513	Vasco Nunez de Balboa	Spain	Panama to the Pacific Ocean
1519	Ferdinand Magellan	Spain	South America
1519	Hernan Cortes	Spain	Mexico
1539	Hernando de Soto	Spain	Mississippi River

THE FIRST SETTLERS

When the first Europeans came to America, they found Native American tribes living there. Many Native Americans lived in large villages. Others moved from place to place.

Taking Native Lands

Some Europeans were looking for a short way across the huge continent. Others wanted land, gold, and furs. When Europeans found land they liked, they bought it from the Native Americans for very little money. Sometimes they took it without paying anything.

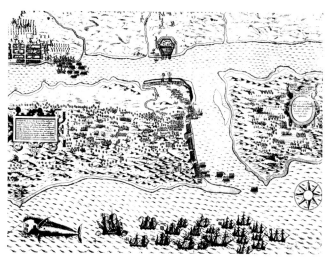

The Spanish colony of St. Augustine, Florida, 1588.

The Native Americans and the settlers fought many battles to decide who owned the land. Many Native Americans also died from diseases brought by the Europeans.

This painting shows Roger Williams buying the land to build Providence, Rhode Island, from the Narrangansett tribe.

European Settlers

Europeans created areas called *colonies* in North America. France had colonies in Canada and along the Mississippi River. Spanish colonies were in Florida, California, and Mexico. The Dutch and English colonies were along the east coast of America. Often the Europeans fought each other. The winner took the loser's land. For example, when the English beat the French, Canada became an English colony.

England took over most of North America after winning the French-Indian war in 1763.

The Thirteen Colonies

The first English colony was Jamestown, Virginia. It was settled in 1607. By 1733 there were thirteen English colonies in America. The colonists disliked many of the laws the English made. They wanted to make their own laws. The American colonies wanted their independence from England.

In December 1773, about 150 colonists dumped chests of British tea into Boston Harbor. This is called the Boston Tea Party.

THE REVOLUTIONARY WAR

England would not give up its colonies without a fight. England sent soldiers to America. In 1775, at Lexington and Concord, Massachusetts, the Americans and English fought the first battles of the Revolutionary War. On July 4, 1776, American leaders signed the Declaration of Independence and created the United States of America.

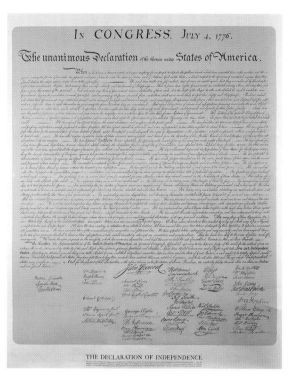

The Declaration of Independence told why the colonists wanted to form their own country.

George Washington

George Washington led the American armies. In his first battle, he forced the English from Boston. Many Americans soon joined the war. Then the English won New York City and Philadelphia. By 1777, it did not look as if the United States would win the war. Washington did not give up. His armies fought until they won a big battle at Yorktown, Virginia, in 1781. The Americans had won the war.

Washington led his army across the Delaware River on Christmas night, 1776.

The Constitution and Bill of Rights

The thirteen states needed a government. The American leaders wrote the Constitution of the United States in 1787, making the laws for the thirteen states. More laws, called the Bill of Rights, were added in 1791.

Slavery

America grew fast. People from Europe and Asia came to America. Many Africans were brought to America as slaves. Most slaves lived in the Southern states. Many Americans wanted slavery to end. The fight over slavery split the United States into two parts, the North and the South.

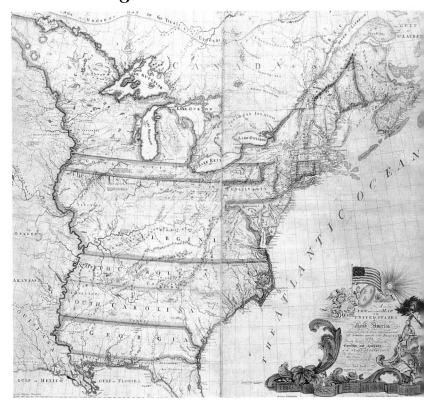

This map of the United States was made by Abel Buell in 1784.

From 1804 to 1806, Lewis and Clark explored America from the Mississippi River to the Pacific Ocean.

CIVIL WAR

In 1860, Abraham Lincoln wanted to be president. The Southern states said that if Lincoln was elected, they would leave the United States. After Lincoln became president, eleven states formed the Confederate States of America. Lincoln wanted to keep the United States together, even if it meant a civil war.

Slaves did most of the work on large cotton farms, called *plantations*.

War Begins

In April 1861, at Fort Sumter, South Carolina, the first shots of the Civil War were fired. Most Americans thought the war would end soon. The first big battle was at Bull Run, near Manassas, Virginia. The South defeated the North. Americans then knew it would be a long war.

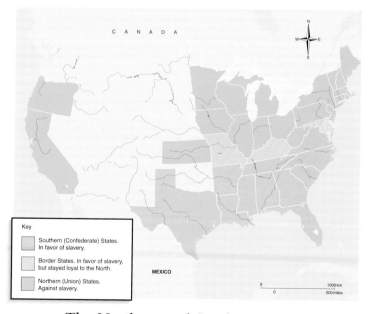

Key

Southern (Confederate) States. In favor of slavery.

Border States. In favor of slavery, but stayed loyal to the North.

Northern (Union) States. Against slavery.

The Northern and Southern states in 1861.

The War and Slavery End

On January 1, 1863, President Lincoln freed the slaves in the Southern states. Slavery had already ended in the North. The Confederate Army, led by General Robert E. Lee, marched north. In July 1863 at Gettysburg, Pennsylvania, Lee's army lost an important battle. Almost two years later, on April 9, 1865, General Lee surrendered.

More than six hundred thousand soldiers died in the Civil War.

After the War

Lincoln wanted to help the Southern states. But on April 14, 1865, he was shot and killed. Andrew Johnson became president. He tried to carry out Lincoln's plans for the South. Many people did not want the slaves to be free. They made laws to keep African Americans and white people apart. They made life difficult for the former slaves.

IMPORTANT DATES

November 1860 ...... Lincoln elected president

December 1860 ...... South Carolina leaves the United States

April 1861 .... Civil War begins

July 1861 .... First Battle of Bull Run

January 1863 .... Emancipation Proclamation frees Southern slaves

July 1863 .... Battle of Gettysburg

November 1863 ...... Lincoln gives Gettysburg Address

April 9, 1865 .... General Lee surrenders

April 15, 1865........ Lincoln dies

May 1865 .... Last Confederate soldiers surrender

December 1865 ...... Slavery outlawed by Thirteenth Amendment to the U.S. Constitution

AMERICA GROWS

After the Civil War, many Americans moved west to settle. Native Americans did not want more people moving into their lands. There were many fights. Sometimes the Native Americans won. Most of the time they lost and were forced off their lands. Their lands then became farms, towns, and cities.

People traveled west in covered wagons.

Settling the West

Railroads were built across America, bringing more people to the West. Herds of cattle grazed on the plains. Some places grew so fast there were few laws to protect people. In many western towns, life was very wild and dangerous.

Cities across the United States, like New York City, were growing.

Industry and Invention

Industry grew quickly. Steel mills made steel for trains and tracks.
Trees were cut down to build cities. New machines helped farmers
grow more crops. Thomas Edison made electric lights. The Wright
Brothers invented the first successful airplane. Henry Ford made
cars cheaper so more people could own them. Millions of
Europeans and Asians moved to America.

About
two million
American
soldiers
were sent
to Europe
during World
War One.

World War One

In 1914, Germany and
Austria-Hungary went to
war against the rest of
Europe. The United States
stayed out of World War One
for three years. The U.S.
joined the war against
Germany in 1917. In 1918,
Germany was defeated. World
War One was over. Millions
of people died in the war.

IMPORTANT DATES

1869 .... First transcontinental railroad finished
1876 .... Native Americans defeat U.S. Army at
                   Battle of Little Big Horn
1879 .... Thomas Edison invents electric light bulb
1903 .... Wilbur and Orville Wright make the first
                   powered airplane flight
1908 .... Henry Ford makes the first Model T car
1914 .... World War One begins
1917 .... America enters World War One
1918 .... World War One ends
1920 .... Nineteenth Amendment to the U.S.
                   Constitution lets women vote

THE WORLD AT WAR

After World War One ended, Americans celebrated. There were many jobs. Farmers grew more crops than ever before. Factories made more cars and many other things for people to buy. It seemed as though the good days would never end.

The Great Depression

In 1929, things changed. Factories closed. People lost their jobs. The weather turned bad and farmers could not grow enough food. People went hungry. Dust storms rolled across the West and many families lost their farms.

During the 1920s, people had fun dancing and listening to jazz.

In the 1930s, huge dust storms covered houses and blew away all the soil needed to grow crops.

World War Two

In Germany, there were many poor people, too. They wanted a strong leader. They chose Adolf Hitler. Hitler wanted to control Europe and rule the world. When Germany attacked Poland in 1939, World War Two began. The German army killed millions of people, including Jews, because of their race or religion.

The War Ends

In Asia, Japan was also taking over other countries. The United States stayed out of the war until Japan bombed U.S. ships and planes at Pearl Harbor in Hawaii. American soldiers fought in Europe, Africa, and Asia from 1941 to 1945.

World War Two was the most destructive war in history.

One atomic bomb destroyed about five square miles of the city of Hiroshima.

Germany surrendered in the spring of 1945. To end the war in Asia, the United States dropped atomic bombs on Hiroshima and Nagasaki, Japan. This powerful new weapon made Japan give up in August 1945.

IMPORTANT DATES

September 1939...... World War Two begins in Europe

December 1941....... Pearl Harbor is bombed. United States enters the war

April 1945 .... Germany surrenders

August 1945........... Japan surrenders

THE 1950S AND 1960S

After World War Two, there were many jobs and plenty of food. But many Americans were not treated fairly. Some laws did not allow African Americans and white children to go to school together. In many places, African Americans could not vote. People like Dr. Martin Luther King Jr. worked hard to change those laws.

Landing on the Moon

Many Americans looked toward the future and into space. In 1969, American astronaut Neil Armstrong became the first person to walk on the moon. Americans have come a long way from those first hunters who crossed the Bering Land Bridge. We have visited the moon and have explored beyond.

Dr. King worked to change unfair laws without using violence.

IMPORTANT DATES

1950–1953 .... Korean War

1957–1973 .... U.S. soldiers in Vietnam War

1964 .... Civil Rights Act gives equal rights to African Americans

1968 .... Dr. Martin Luther King Jr. killed

1969 .... Neil Armstrong is the first person on the moon

The United States landed six spacecraft on the moon from 1969 to 1972.

How to Use This Index Volume

The Subject List (pages 18–22)

The Subject List groups together all entry words in the encyclopedia on a particular subject. For example, under the subject heading DINOSAURS, you will find a list of all the different dinosaur entries in alphabetical order in the whole encyclopedia. The ANIMALS subject list is also divided into types of animals, such as mammals, birds, and fish. The COUNTRIES entries are listed under the continent each country is found in. The main subject headings are in Dewey Decimal order, like books are arranged in most libraries.

The Index (pages 23–32)

The Index lists all the entry words in the encyclopedia and also some other important words. It tells the encyclopedia volume and page number of where the information can be found. Some of the indexed words have *see also* references. These tell you other words to look under in the index to find more information. If the word you look under is not used as an entry in this encyclopedia, there will be a *see* reference to tell under what word to look.

Remember: the volume number is followed by a colon (:) and then by the page number.

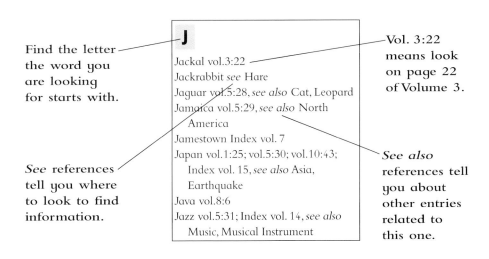

Find the letter the word you are looking for starts with.

J

Jackal vol.3:22
Jackrabbit *see* Hare
Jaguar vol.5:28, *see also* Cat, Leopard
Jamaica vol.5:29, *see also* North America
Jamestown Index vol.7
Japan vol.1:25; vol.5:30; vol.10:43; Index vol.15, *see also* Asia, Earthquake
Java vol.8:6
Jazz vol.5:31; Index vol.14, *see also* Music, Musical Instrument

Vol. 3:22 means look on page 22 of Volume 3.

See also references tell you about other entries related to this one.

See references tell you where to look to find information.

The Subject List

The main subject headings are in Dewey Decimal order, like books in libraries.

WORLD RELIGIONS   200
Buddhism
Christianity
Hinduism
Islam
Judaism
Sikhism

TRANSPORTATION   300
Airplane
Balloon
Barge
Bicycle
Bus
Canoe
Car
Helicopter
Hovercraft
Motorcycle
Railroad
Road
Ship
Spacecraft
Submarine
Train
Truck
Waterway

ANIMALS   500

Amphibians
Frog
Toad

Birds
Chicken
Crane
Duck
Eagle
Emu
Flamingo
Goose
Gull
Hawk
Hummingbird
Kiwi
Ostrich
Owl
Parrot
Penguin
Pigeon
Seabird
Swan
Vulture
Woodpecker

Arachnids
Scorpion
Spider

PLANTS   500
Cactus
Fern
Flower
Forest
Fungus
Leaf
Moss
Root
Seed
Stem
Tree
Wood

DINOSAURS   500
Brachiosaurus
Pterosaur
Stegosaurus
Triceratops
Tyrannosaurus

Crustaceans
Crab
Woodlouse

Fish/Sea Animals
Eel
Coral
Fish, Tropical
Jellyfish
Ray
Sea Anemone
Sea Horse
Sea Urchin
Shark
Starfish

Insects
Ant
Bee
Beetle
Butterfly
Caterpillar
Cockroach
Dragonfly
Earwig
Firefly
Flea
Fly
Grasshopper
Ladybug
Lice
Mosquito
Moth
Praying Mantis
Termite
Wasp

ANIMALS (CONT'D)

Mammals

Aardvark	Coyote	Koala	Raccoon
Anteater	Deer	Leopard	Rat
Antelope	Dog	Lion	Rhinoceros
Ape	Dolphin	Marsupial	Sea Lion
Badger	Elephant	Monkey	Seal
Bat	Fox	Moose	Sheep
Bear	Giraffe	Mouse	Skunk
Beaver	Goat	Opossum	Squirrel
Bison	Hare	Otter	Tiger
Buffalo	Hedgehog	Panda	Whale
Camel	Hippopotamus	Pig	Wolf
Cat	Horse	Platypus	Wolverine
Cattle	Jaguar	Porcupine	Zebra
Cheetah	Kangaroo	Rabbit	

Mollusks

Octopus	Snail
Slug	Squid

Reptiles

Alligator	Snake
Crocodile	Tortoise
Lizard	Turtle

Nocturnal Animals

Aardvark	Coyote		
Badger	Earwig	Hedgehog	Owl
Bat	Firefly	Hippopotamus	Rabbit
Cat	Fox	Kiwi	Raccoon
Centipede	Frog	Koala	Slug
Cockroach	Hare	Moth	Toad
		Opossum	

WEATHER 500

Air	Hurricane	Tornado
Climate	Lightning	Rainbow
Water Cycle	Flood	Seasons

SCIENCE AND TECHNOLOGY   500 AND 600

Air
Bacteria
Bar
Code
Blood
Calendar
Camera
Color
Comet
Communication
Computer
Day and Night
Drug
Ear
Egg
Electricity
Endangered Species
Energy
Engine
Eye
Food Chain

Fuel
Heart
Hibernation
Human Body
Internet
Laser
Life Cycle
Light
Lung
Machines, Simple
Magnet
Matter
Measurement
Metal
Metamorphosis
Meteor
Migration
Moon
Nutrition
Oxygen
Photosynthesis

Planets
Plastic
Pollution
Radio
Robot
Skeleton
Smell
Soil
Solar System
Sound
Space Exploration
Star
Sun
Taste
Telephone
Television
Time
Tooth
Touch
Virus

THE ARTS   700

Arts
Architecture
Painting
Sculpture

Literature
Fable
Fairy Tale
Language
Legend
Myth
Poetry
Story

Music
Classical Music
Folk Music
Jazz
Musical Instruments
Orchestra
Percussion Instruments
Pop Music
Stringed Instruments
Wind Instruments

Performing Arts
Ballet
Dance
Drama
Opera
Puppetry
Theater

GEOGRAPHY 900

Aborigines
Africa
Antarctica
Arctic
Asia
Australia and Oceania
Bay
Coast
Continent
Crop
Delta
Desert
Earth
Earthquake
Europe
Farming
Home
Island
Lake
Map
Mining
Mountain
North America
Ocean
Peninsula
Port
Rainforest
River
Rocks
Seasons
South America
Tundra
Valley
Volcano
Water

COUNTRIES 900

Africa

Algeria
Botswana
Chad
Democratic Republic
    of Congo
Egypt
Ethiopia
Ghana
Kenya
Libya
Madagascar
Morocco
Nigeria
Rwanda
Somalia
South Africa
Sudan
Tunisia
Uganda
Zambia
Zimbabwe

Asia

Afghanistan
Bangladesh
Cambodia
China
India
Indonesia
Iran
Iraq
Israel
Japan
Jordan
Kuwait
Laos
Lebanon
Malaysia
Nepal
North Korea
Pakistan
Philippines
Russia
Saudi Arabia
Singapore

Asia (CONT'D)

South Korea
Sri Lanka
Syria
Taiwan
Thailand
Turkey
Vietnam

Australia and Oceania

Australia
New Zealand
Papua New Guinea

COUNTRIES
(CONT'D)

Europe
Albania
Austria
Belgium
Bosnia-
  Herzegovina
Bulgaria
Croatia
Czech Republic
Denmark
England
Finland
France
Germany
Greece
Hungary
Iceland
Ireland
Italy
Luxembourg

Europe (CONT'D)
Netherlands
Northern Ireland
Norway
Poland
Portugal
Romania
Russia
Scotland
Slovakia
Slovenia
Spain
Sweden
Switzerland
Turkey
Ukraine
United Kingdom
Wales
Yugoslavia

North America
Bahamas
Barbados
Belize
Canada
Costa Rica
Cuba
Dominican
  Republic
El Salvador
Guatemala
Haiti
Honduras
Jamaica
Mexico
Nicaragua
Panama
Puerto Rico
United States
  of America

South America
Argentina
Bolivia
Brazil
Chile
Colombia
Ecuador
Peru
Trinidad and
  Tobago
Venezuela

HISTORY 900

Alphabet
Aztecs
Bronze Age
Castle
Cathedral
China, Ancient
Egypt, Ancient
Flag
Fossil
Greece, Ancient

Hieroglyphics
Incas
Industrial Revolution
Iron Age
Knight
Maya
Middle Ages
Money
Native Americans

Olympic Games
Pyramid
Rome, Ancient
Stone Age
United Nations
Vikings
World War One
World War Two

The Index

*Remember, the volume number is followed
by a colon(:), and then by the page number.*

A

Aardvark vol.1:4; *see also* Anteater,
  Mammal
Aardwolf vol.3:15
Abacus vol.7:11
Aborigines vol.1:5; vol.6:44, 45;
  vol.10:36; *see also* Australia,
  Australia and Oceania
Abstract Painting vol.1:24;
  vol.7:23
Acid Rain vol.7:43
Acropolis vol.4:35
Aesop vol.4:5
Afghanistan vol.1:6; *see also* Asia
Africa vol.1:7; vol.2:47; vol.5:4, 43;
  see also Continent, Desert
African Americans Index:11, 16
Air Pollution vol.7:43
Air vol.1:8; *see also* Oxygen,
  Pollution
Airplane vol.1:9; vol.9:11; Index:13;
  see also Helicopter, Transportation
Albania vol.1:10; *see also* Europe
Albatross vol.8:36
Algeria vol.1:11; *see also* Africa,
  Desert
Allah vol. 5:24
Alligator vol.1:12; vol.3:9; vol.8:16;
  see also Crocodile, Reptile
Alloy vol. 6:24
Alpaca vol.7:32
Alphabet vol.1:13; vol.2:7; vol.3:17;
  vol.4:35, 46; *see also* Hieroglyphics,
  Language
Aluminum vol.6:16, 24
Amazon Rainforest vol.2:10; vol.4:21;
  vol.8:13; vol.9:13
Amazon River vol. 8:18; vol. 9:13
American History Index:4–16; *see also*
  United States of America
Amphibian vol.1:14; vol. 3:36;
  vol.6:6; *see also* Frog,
  Metamorphosis, Toad
Amphitheater vol. 9:42
Amundsen, Roald vol.1:17

Andersen, Hans Christian
  vol.3:19, vol.4:6
Andes Mountains vol.1:23;
  vol.2:6, 42; vol.3:34; vol.7:32
  vol.9:13; vol.10:22
Animals vol.1:15; vol.4:20, 45;
  vol.7:22, *see also* Invertebrate,
  Vertebrate
Ant vol.1:16; *see also* Aardvark,
  Anteater, Insect
Antarctica vol.1:17; vol.2:47; vol.7:13;
  see also Continent
Anteater vol.1:18; vol.6:18; *see also*
  Aardvark, Mammal
Antelope vol.1:19; *see also* Mammal
Ape vol.1:20; *see also* Mammal,
  Monkey
Appleseed, Johnny vol.5:47
Aquarium vol.4:12
Arabia vol.7:30
Architecture vol.1:21; *see also* Art,
  Castle, Cathedral, Home
Arctic vol.1:22; vol. 8:25; *see also*
  Tundra
Arctic Ocean vol.5:12; vol.7:13
Argentina vol.1:23; *see also* South
  America
Armor vol.5:38
Armstrong, Louis vol.5:31
Armstrong, Neil vol.6:34; Index:16
Art vol.1:24; *see also* Architecture,
  Painting, Sculpture
Artificial Intelligence vol.8:20
Asia vol.1:25; vol.2:47; *see also*
  Continent
Asteroid vol.9:9
Astronaut vol.9:16
Athlete vol.3:44
Atlantic Ocean vol.3:48;
  vol.5:12; vol.7:7, 13, 25;
  vol.9:13
Atmosphere vol.3:31
Atom vol.6:21
Atomic Bomb vol.10:43; Index:15
Atomic Clock vol.9:44

Australia vol. 1:26; *see also* Aborigines,
  Australia and Oceania, Marsupial
Australia and Oceania vol.1:27; *see
  also* Aborigines, Continent,
  Marsupial
Austria vol.1:28; *see also* Europe
Autumn vol.8:38
Aztecs vol.1:29; vol.4:46; *see also*
  Maya, Mexico

B

Babbage, Charles vol.2:46
Bach, Johann Sebastian vol.2:38
Bacteria vol.1:30; vol.9:46;
  see also Virus
Badger vol.1:31; *see also* Mammal
Bagpipes vol.10:36
Bahamas vol.1:32; *see also* Island,
  North America
Ballet vol.1:33; vol.3:14; *see also*
  Dance
Balloon vol.1:34; *see also* Airplane,
  Transportation
Bamboo vol.7:26; vol.9:25
Banana vol.1:46; vol.3:4, 18
Bangladesh vol.1:35; *see also* Asia
Bar Code vol.1:36; *see also*
  Computer, Laser
Barbados vol.1:37; *see also* Hurricane,
  North America
Barge vol.1:38; vol.10:33; *see also*
  River, Transportation, Waterway
Basketball vol.7:33
Bat vol.1:39; vol.4:45; *see also*
  Mammal
Bay vol.1:40; *see also* Coast, Lake,
  Ocean, Port
Beach vol.2:40
Beans vol.3:37, 39
Bear vol.1:25, 41; vol.4:45;
  see also Mammal
Beaver vol.1:42; *see also* Mammal
Bedouin vol.5:33
Bee vol.1:43; *see also* Insect

Beetle vol.1:44; vol.5:17; *see also* Earwig, Insect

Belgium vol.1:45; *see also* Europe

Belize vol.1:46; *see also* Maya, North America

Bell, Alexander Graham vol.2:45, vol.9:38

Bering Land Bridge Index:4

Bible vol.2:18, 37

Bicycle vol.1:47; *see also* Motorcycle, Transportation

Bidpai vol.4:5

Bill of Rights Index:9

Bird vol.1:48; vol.3:36; vol. 6:6, 29; *see also* Animals, Seabird

Bird of prey vol.3:29; vol.4:40; vol.7:21

Bison vol.2:4; vol.6:46; *see also* Buffalo, Mammal

Black Sea vol.2:14; vol.10:17

Blood vol.2:5; vol.4:41; *see also* Heart, Human Body

Blood donor vol.2:5

Blue whale vol.6:18

Bohemia *see* Czech Republic

Bolivia vol.2:6; *see also* South America

Bombay vol.5:14

Bone vol.3:30; vol.8:45; vol.10:23

Borneo vol.6:17

Bosnia-Herzegovina vol.2:7; *see also* Europe, Yugoslavia

Boston Tea Party Index:7

Botswana vol.2:8; *see also* Africa

Brachiosaurus vol.2:9; vol.3:21; *see also* Dinosaur, Fossil

Braille vol.10:4

Bratislava vol.8:47

Brazil vol.2:10; *see also* Rainforest, South America

Breathing vol.5:8; vol.6:12

Bronze vol.2:11; vol.5:23; vol.6:24

Bronze Age vol.2:11; *see also* Iron Age, Stone Age

Buddhism vol.2:12; vol.5:14; vol.9:41; *see also* India

Buffalo vol.2:13; vol.9:41; *see also* Bison, Mammal

Bulgaria vol.2:14; *see also* Europe

Bus vol.2:15; *see also* Transportation

Butterfly vol.2:16, 27; vol. 4:45; vol.6:25; *see also* Caterpillar, Metamorphosis

C

Cactus vol.2:17; vol.3:20; *see also* Desert, Plants

Calcutta vol.5:14

Calendar vol.2:18; *see also* Seasons, Time

Calorie vol.7:12

Cambodia vol.2:19; *see also* Asia

Camel vol.2:20; *see also* Desert, Mammal

Camera vol.2:21; *see also* Light

Canada vol.2:22; vol. 3:15; Index:6; *see also* North America

Canal vol.1:38; vol.10:33

Canoe vol.2:23; *see also* Native Americans, Transportation

Canyon vol.10:21

Cape Cod vol. 7:30

Cape Town vol. 1:7

Car vol.2:24, 46; vol.3:45; Index:13, 14; *see also* Engine, Transportation

Caracas vol.10:22

Carat vol. 6:23

Carbon dioxide vol.1:8; vol.6:12; vol.7:22

Cargo ship vol.7:46; vol.8:42

Caribbean Sea vol.7:7

Caribou vol.1:22; vol.3:16

Carnivore vol.1:15; vol.4:20; vol.9:46

Carthage vol.10:12

Cartilage vol.10:23

Castle vol.2:25; *see also* Middle Ages

Cat vol.2:26; *see also* Cheetah, Jaguar, Leopard, Lion, Tiger

Caterpillar vol.2:16, 27; vol.6:25,39; *see also* Butterfly, Metamorphosis, Moth

Catfish vol.10:4

Cathedral vol.2:28; *see also* Christianity, Middle Ages

Cattle vol.2:29; *see also* Farming; Mammal

CD player vol.5:44

CD-ROM vol.2:46

Centipede vol.2:30; *see also* Invertebrate

Ceylon *see* Sri Lanka

Chad vol.2:31; *see also* Africa

Chalk vol.4:22; vol.8:21

Chameleon vol.6:11

Chart vol.6:19

Check vol.6:32

Cheetah vol.2:32; *see also* Cat, Mammal

Chewing gum vol.4:36

Chicken vol.2:33; *see also* Bird

Chile vol.2;34; vol.5:13; *see also* South America

Chimpanzee vol.1:20

China vol.1:47; vol.2:35; *see also* Asia, China, Ancient

China, Ancient vol.2:36; *see also* China

Chinese opera vol.7:16

Chlorophyll vol.5:45; vol.7:34

Chocolate vol. 1:45; vol. 4:29

Choreographer vol.1:33

Christianity vol.2:37; vol.4:38; vol.6:28; *see also* Cathedral, Israel, Judaism

Chrysalis vol.6:25,39

Circulatory System vol.5:8

City-State vol. 4:35

Civil War, American Index:10-11

Clam vol.6:31

Clarinet vol.10:36

Classical Music vol.2:38; vol.7:18; *see also* Music, Musical Instruments

Clay vol.9:8

Climate vol.2:39; *see also* Seasons, Weather

Clock vol. 9:44

Coal vol.3:40, 44; vol.4:22, 26; vol.5:16; vol.6:30

Coast vol.2:40; *see also* Bay, Delta

Cocaine vol. 3:27

Cockroach vol.2:41; *see also* Insect

Cocoa vol.4:29

Cod vol.3:36

Coffee vol.2:42; vol.3:4, 47

Colombia vol.2:42; *see also* South America

Colonies Index:6-7

Color vol.2:43; vol.8:12; *see also* Light

Columbus, Christopher vol.3:12, 24; vol.10:22; Index:4, 5

Comedy vol.3:26

Comet vol.2:44; vol.6:26; vol. 9:9; *see also* Solar System

Commonwealth vol.10:18

Communication vol.2:45; *see also* Computer, Internet, Radio, Telephone, Television

Commuter vol.10:6

Composer vol. 2:38; vol. 7:16,18

Computer vol.1:36; vol.2:46; vol.5:18; vol.6:36; vol. 7:11; vol.8:20; *see also* Bar Code, Laser

Condor vol.9:13

Conductor (heat) vol. 4:42; vol. 6:24

Conductor (orchestra) vol.7:18

Confucius vol.7:8

Coniferous Tree vol. 4:21; vol. 10:7

Consonant vol.1:13

Constellation vol.9:22

Constitution, American Index:9

Continent vol.2:47; *see also* Earth, Ocean

Copernicus vol.9:9

Copper vol.2:11; vol.6:24,30; vol.10:46

Coral vol.2:48; vol.6:15; vol.8:33; *see also* Coast, Island

Cormorant vol.8:36

Corn vol. 2:42; vol. 3:10; vol. 5:5

Costa Rica vol.3:4; *see also* North America

Costume, Traditional *see* entries for individual countries

Cotton vol.3:10; vol.5:16

Coyote vol.3:5, 22; *see also* Dog, Mammal, Wolf

Crab vol.3:6, 11; vol.5:19; vol.8:33; *see also* Crustacean, Invertebrate, Sea Life

Crafts *see* entries for individual countries

Crane vol.3:7; *see also* Bird

Crater vol.6:26, 34

Credit card vol.6:32

Creole vol.1:46; vol.4:38

Croatia vol.3:8; *see also* Europe, Yugoslavia

Crocodile vol.1:27; vol.3:9, 36; vol.8:16; *see also* Alligator, Reptile

Crop vol.3:10; vol.4:7; vol.8:38; vol.10:21; *see also* Farming, and entries for individual countries and crops

Crustacean vol.3:11; vol.8:33; *see also* Animals, Invertebrate, Sea Life

Cuba vol.3:12; *see also* Island, North America

Cuneiform Writing vol.6:10

Current vol. 7:13

Cuttlefish vol. 6:17, 31

Cyrillic alphabet vol.2:7

Czech Republic vol.3:13; *see also* Europe, Slovakia

Czechoslovakia *see* Slovakia, Czech Republic

D

da Vinci, Leonardo vol.7:23

Dam vol.3:40; vol.4:16; vol.10:31

Dance vol.3:14; *see also* Ballet, Music

Danube River vol. 5:10; vol.8:22

Day and Night vol.3:15; *see also* Seasons

Dead Sea vol. 5:33

Death Valley vol. 7:7

Deciduous Tree vol. 4:21

Decimal vol. 7:11

Declaration of Independence Index:8

Deer vol.3:16; *see also* Antelope, Mammal, Moose

Delta vol.3:17; *see also* Coast, River

Democratic Republic of Congo (DRC) vol.3:18; *see also* Africa

Denmark vol.3:19; *see also* Europe

Desert vol. 2:39; vol.3:20; vol.8:38; *see also* Cactus, Camel, Climate

Diamond vol.6:23, 30

Didgeridoo vol.10:36

Diesel engine vol.10:5, 10

Digestive system vol.5:8

Dingo vol.1:27; vol.3:22

Dinosaur vol.3:21; vol.4:22; *see also* Fossil, Reptile

Disease vol.4:18, 27; vol.6:37; vol.8:14; vol.10:26

Dog vol.3:22; vol.9:5; vol.10:23; *see also* Coyote, Mammal, Wolf

Dolphin vol.3:23; *see also* Mammal, Whale

Dominican Republic vol.3:24; *see also* Island, North America

Dove vol.7:36

Dracula vol.8:22

Dragonfly vol.3:25; *see also* Insect

Drama vol.3:26; *see also* Literature

Dreamtime vol.1:5

Drought vol.3:47

Drug vol.3:27

Drum vol.7:31

Duck vol.3:28; vol.8:36; *see also* Bird, Goose, Swan

Dung beetle vol.1:44

Dust Storm Index:14

E

E-mail (electronic mail) vol.2:45; vol.5:18; vol.9:38

Eagle vol.3:29; *see also* Bird, Hawk

Ear vol.3:30; *see also* Human Body, Sound

Earth vol.3:15, 31; vol.6:7, 16; vol.7:37; vol.9:9; *see also* Planets, Solar System, Weather

Earthquake vol.3:32; vol.5:30; vol.7:5, 32; *see also* Earth

Earwig vol.3:33; *see also* Insect

Echo vol.9:11

Echolocation vol. 1:39; vol.3:23

Ecuador vol.3:34; vol.5:13; *see also* Incas, South America

Edison, Thomas Index:13

Eel vol.3:35; *see also* Fish

Egg vol.3:36; vol.6:6; *see also* Bird, and entries for individual animals

Egypt vol.3:37; *see also* Africa; Egypt, Ancient; Pyramid

Egypt, Ancient vol.3:38; vol.4:46; vol.6:23; vol.8:7, 42; *see also* Egypt, Hieroglyphics, Pyramid

Eiffel Tower vol.4:24

Eire *see* Ireland

El Salvador vol.3:39; *see also* North America

Electricity vol.3:40, 44, 45; vol.4:26; vol.6:7, 8, 24, 41; vol.8:18; vol.10:31, 32, 34; Index:13; *see also* Energy, Heat, Light

Electronic keyboard vol.6:44; vol.7:18

Elephant vol.3:30, 41; *see also* Mammal

Emu vol.3:42; *see also* Australia, Bird

Endangered Species vol.3:43; *see also* Animals, Plants

Energy vol.3:44; vol. 4:26; vol.6:7, 8; vol.7:12; vol.10:32; *see also* Electricity, Heat, Light, Sound

Engine vol.3:45; 10:5, 10; *see also* Car, Electricity, Transportation

England vol.3:46; Index:6, 7, 8; *see also* Northern Ireland, Scotland, United Kingdom, Wales

English Language vol.5:43

Erosion vol.2:40; vol.9:8

Ethiopia vol.3:47; vol.5:4; *see also* Africa

Eucalyptus vol.4:21; vol.5:39

Europe vol.2:47; vol.3:48; *see also* Continent

European Union (EU) vol. 3:48

Exoskeleton vol.8:45

Eye vol.4:4; *see also* Animals, Human Body

F

Fable vol.4:5; *see also* Legend, Literature, Myth, Story

Fairy Tale vol.4:6; *see also* Fable, Literature, Myth, Story

Farming vol.4:7; vol.8:38; vol.9:8; vol.10:21; Index:13, 14; *see also* Crop, Soil, Weather, and entries for individual countries

Fax vol.2:45; vol.9:38

Feather vol.1:48

Fern vol.4:8, 21; *see also* Plants

Ferry vol 8:42

Fertilizer vol.3:10; vol.4:7; vol.9:8

Festivals *see* Calendar, and entries for individual countries and religions

Finland vol.4:9; *see also* Arctic, Europe

Firefly vol.4:10; *see also* Beetle, Insect

Fish vol.4:11; *see also* Fish, Tropical; Sea Life

Fish, Tropical vol.4:12; *see also* Coral, Fish, Sea Life

Fishing vol.2:40; vol.5:12

Flag vol.4:13; vol. 8:27; *see also* Communication

Flamingo vol.4:14; *see also* Bird

Flax vol.1:45; vol.3:10; vol.7:9

Flea vol.4:15; *see also* Insect

Flood vol.3:17; vol.4:16; *see also* Delta, River, Weather

Florida Index:5

Flower vol.4:17; *see also* Leaf, Plants, Root, Seed, Stem

Fly vol.4:18; *see also* Insect, Mosquito

Folk Music vol.4:19; *see also* Music, Musical Instruments

Fontaine, Jean de la vol.4:5

Food *see* entries for individual countries

Food Chain vol.4:20; *see also* Animals, Plants

Food Guide Pyramid vol. 7:12

Food Poisoning vol.4:18

Ford, Henry Index:13

Forest vol.4:21; vol.10:7; *see also* Rainforest, Tree, Wood

Formosa *see* Taiwan

Fossil vol.4:22; *see also* Dinosaur, Fuel

Fossil Fuel vol.4:22, 26

Fox vol.4:23; *see also* Dog, Coyote, Wolf

France vol.4:24; *see also* Europe

Franklin, Benjamin vol.6:8

French horn vol.10:36

French Revolution vol.4:24

Frequency vol.8:10

Frog vol.1:14; vol.4:25, 45, *see also* Amphibian, Metamorphosis, Toad

Fuel vol. 3:45; 4:26, 42; *see also* Electricity, Energy, Fossil

Fungus vol.4:27; *see also* Plants

G

Galapagos Islands vol. 3:34

Galaxy vol.9:22

Ganges River vol. 1:25; vol. 3:17; vol. 5:14

Gas vol.6:21

Gas, Natural vol.3:40; vol.4:26; vol.5:40; vol.6:4, 7, 30; vol.7:10

Gasoline vol. 3:45; vol. 4:26

Gaucho vol. 1:23

Gecko vol.8:16

German Democratic Republic *see* Germany

German Federal Republic *see* Germany

Germany vol.4:28; vol.10:42, 43; Index:13, 15; *see also* Europe

Gettysburg Index:11

Geyser vol. 5:12

Ghana vol.4:29; *see also* Africa

Gibbon vol.1:20

Gilbert and Sullivan vol.7:16

Gillespie, Dizzy vol.6:43

Giraffe vol.4:30; *see also* Mammal

Glacier vol.5:12

Glass vol.3:13

Globe vol.6:19

Globe Theater vol.9:42

Glowworm vol.4:10

Goat vol.4:31; *see also* Mammal

Gods and Goddesses vol.1:29; vol.3:38; vol.4:35, 47; vol.5:13; vol.6:22, 45; vol.10:25

Gold vol.6:24, 30; Index:5, 6

Gold Coast vol.4:29

Goose vol.4:32; vol.8:36; *see also* Bird

Gorge vol.10:21

Gorilla vol.1:20; vol.8:26

Gourd vol. 4:38

Grain vol. 8:39

Grand Canyon vol. 10:20, 21

Grasshopper vol.3:30; vol.4:33; vol.6:6, 25; *see also* Insect

Gravity vol.9:9, 31

Great Britain vol.10:18

Great Depression Index:14

Great Rift Valley vol. 5:42

Great Salt Lake vol. 5:42

Great Wall of China vol.2:35, 36

Greece vol.4:34; *see also* Europe; Greece, Ancient

Greece, Ancient vol.4:35; vol.6:45; vol.7:15; vol.8:30; vol.9:42; *see also* Greece, Olympic Games

Greek alphabet vol.3:17

Greenland vol.1:22; vol.5:25

Grimm Brothers vol.4:6

Guatemala vol.4:36; *see also* North America

Guitar vol.6:44; vol.9:28

Gulf States vol.5:40

Gulf Stream vol.5:12; vol.7:13

Gulf War vol.5:21

Gull vol.4:37; vol.8:36; vol.10:23; *see also* Bird, Seabird

Guru Granth Sahib vol. 8:43

Guru Nanak vol.8:43

H

Hailstone vol.10:34

Haiti vol.4:38; *see also* North America

Hale-Bopp comet vol.2:44

Haley, Bill vol.7:44

Halley's Comet vol.2:44

Hare vol.4:39; *see also* Mammal, Rabbit

Hawaiian Islands vol.5:25

Hawk vol.4:40; *see also* Bird

Heart vol.2:5; vol.4:41; vol.5:8; *see also* Blood, Human Body

Heat vol.3:44; vol.4:42; *see also* Energy, Fuel

Hedgehog vol.4:43, 45; *see also* Hibernation, Mammal

Helicopter vol.4:44; *see also* Airplane, Transportation

Helvetia vol. 9:34

Hendrix, Jimi vol.6:44

Herbivore vol.1:15; vol.4:20; vol.9:46

Herzegovina *see* Bosnia-Herzegovina

Hibernation vol.1:39, 41; vol.4:45; vol.8:38; *see also* Animals, Seasons

Hieroglyphics vol.1:29; vol.3:38; vol.4:46; vol.6:22; *see also* Alphabet; Aztecs; Egypt, Ancient; Maya

Highland Games vol. 8:29

Himalaya Mountains vol.1:25; vol.2:35; vol.5:14; vol.6:41, 47

Hinduism vol.4:47; vol.5:14; vol.6:47; *see also* India

Hippopotamus vol.4:48; *see also* Mammal

Hispaniola vol.3:24; vol.4:38

Hitler, Adolf vol.10:43; Index:15

HIV and AIDS vol. 10:26

Ho Chi Minh City vol. 10:24

Holland *see* Netherlands

Holocaust vol.5:34

Hologram vol.5:44

Home vol.5:4; *see also* Architecture

Honduras vol.5:5; *see also* North America

Honey vol.1:43

Hong Kong vol.1:25

Hornet vol.10:30

Horse vol.5:6; *see also* Mammal, Transportation

Hovercraft vol.5:7; *see also* Transportation

Human Body vol.5:8; vol.10:31; *see also* Blood, Heart, Lung

Hummingbird vol.3:36; vol.5:9; *see also* Bird, Migration

Hungary vol.5:10; *see also* Europe

Hurricane vol.1:37; vol.5:11; vol.10:34; *see also* Tornado, Weather

Hutu vol.8:26

Hydroelectric power vol.10:32

I

Ice vol.6:21

Iceberg vol. 7:13

Iceland vol.5:12; *see also* Europe, Island

Iguana vol.6:11

Immunization vol.10:26

Incas vol.5:13; *see also* Aztecs, Maya, South America

India vol.5:14; vol.6:43; *see also* Asia

Indian Ocean vol.1:7, 40; vol.7:13

Indonesia vol.1:25; vol.5:15; vol.7:18; *see also* Asia

Indus River vol. 7:24

Industrial Revolution vol.5:16; *see also* United Kingdom

Industry *see* entries for individual countries

Insect vol.4:45; vol.5:17, 19; vol.6:6, 25; *see also* Animals, Invertebrate, Metamorphosis

Insectivore vol.1:15

Insulation vol.3:44; vol.4:42

Internal Combustion Engine vol.3:45

Internet vol.5:18; vol.6:10; vol.9:38; *see also* Communication, Computer, Telephone

Inuit vol.2:23; vol.10:11

Invertebrate vol.5:19; *see also* Crustacean, Insect, Mollusk, Vertebrate

Iran vol.5:20, 21; *see also* Asia, Islam

Iraq vol.5:21; *see also* Asia

Ireland vol.5:22; *see also* Europe, Northern Ireland

Iron Age vol.5:23; *see also* Bronze Age, Stone Age

Islam vol.5:20, 24, 33; vol.7:24; vol.8:27; vol.9:35

Island vol.5:25; *see also* Coast, Coral, Ocean

Israel vol.5:26; *see also* Asia

Italy vol.5:27; vol.7:30; *see also* Europe; Rome, Ancient

J

Jackal vol.3:22

Jackrabbit *see* Hare

Jaguar vol.5:28; *see also* Cat, Leopard

Jamaica vol.5:29; *see also* North America

Jamestown Index:7

Japan vol.1:25; vol.5:30; vol.10:43; Index:15; *see also* Asia, Earthquake

Java vol.8:6

Jazz vol.5:31; Index:14; *see also* Music, Musical Instrument

Jellyfish vol.5:19, 32; *see also* Invertebrate, Sea Life

Jerusalem vol.5:26, 34

Jesus Christ vol.2:37

Jews vol.5:26; Index:15; *see also* Judaism

Johnson, Andrew Index:11

Jordan vol.5:33; *see also* Asia

Judaism vol.5:34; *see also* Israel

Jupiter vol.7:37; vol.9:9

Jute vol. 1:35

K

Kalahari Desert vol.1:7; vol.2:8; vol.3:20

Kangaroo vol.1:27; vol.5:35; vol.6:20; *see also* Australia and Oceania, Mammal, Marsupial

Karakoram Mountains vol.6:41

Kenya vol.5:36; *see also* Africa

King Arthur vol.5:47

King Jr., Martin Luther Index:16

Kiwi vol.1:27; vol.5:37; vol.7:4; *see also* Bird, New Zealand

Knight vol.5:38; *see also* Middle Ages

Koala vol.1:27; vol.5:39; *see also* Australia and Oceania, Mammal, Marsupial

Komodo Dragon vol.5:15; vol.6:11

Koran vol. 5:24

Krill vol.1:17; vol.7:29; vol.8:40

Kuwait vol.5:21, 40; *see also* Asia, Desert

L

Ladybug vol.5:41; *see also* Beetle, Insect

Lake vol.5:42; *see also* River, Valley

Language vol.5:43; *see also* Alphabet, Communication, and entries for individual countries

Lapland vol.4:9

Lapps vol.10:11

Laser vol.1:36; vol.5:44; *see also* Bar Code, Computer; Light

Lava vol.10:27

Leaf vol.5:45; vol.7:34; *see also* Photosynthesis, Plants

Lebanon vol.5:46; *see also* Asia

Lee, Robert E. Index:11

Leech vol.10:44

Legend vol.5:47; *see also* Literature, Myth, Story

Lemur vol.6:15

Leopard vol.5:48; *see also* Cat, Jaguar, Mammal

Lessing, Gotthold Ephraim vol.4:5

Lever vol.6:14

Libya vol.6:4; *see also* Africa, Desert

Lice vol. 3:11; vol. 6:5; *see also* Insect

Life cycle vol.6:6; *see also* Flower, Metamorphosis

Light vol.3:40, 44; vol.6:7, 34; vol.9:22; *see also* Color, Energy, Sun

Light pollution vol.7:43

Lightning vol.6:8; vol.10:34; *see also* Electricity, Weather

Lincoln, Abraham Index:10, 11

Lion vol.4:20; vol.6:9; *see also* Africa, Cat, Mammal

Liquid vol.6:21

Literature vol.6:10; *see also* Drama, Poetry, Story

Litter vol. 7:43

Little Mermaid vol. 3:19

Livingstone, David vol.10:46

Lizard vol.1:15; vol.6:11; vol.8:16; *see also* Reptile

Llama vol.3:34

Llanos vol. 10:22

Lobster vol.3:11; vol.5:19

Loch Ness vol.5:42; vol.8:29

Lock vol. 10:33

Locust vol.5:17

London vol.3:46; vol.10:18, 43

Longfellow, Henry Wadsworth vol.7:41

Longhouse vol.6:46; vol.7:33

Longship vol.10:25

Lung vol.5:8; vol.6:12; *see also* Air, Human Body, Oxygen

Luxembourg vol.6:13; *see also* Europe

M

Machines, Simple vol.6:14; *see also* Energy

Machu Picchu vol.5:13

Madagascar vol.6:15; *see also* Africa, Island

Maggot vol.4:18

Magma vol.8:21; vol.10:27

Magnet vol.6:16

Malaria vol.4:18

Malaysia vol.6:17; *see also* Asia, Rainforest

Malnutrition vol.7:12

Mammal vol.3:36; vol.6:18; *see also* Animals, Vertebrate

Mandela, Nelson vol.9:12

Manta ray vol.8:15

Maori vol.6:45; vol.7:4

Map vol.6:19

Marconi, Guglielmo vol.8:10

Mariana Trench vol.7:13

Marionette vol.8:6

Mars vol.7:37; vol.9:9, 15; vol.10:27

Marsh Arabs vol.5:21

Marsupial vol.6:20; *see also* Australia, Kangaroo, Koala, Mammal, Opossum

Matter vol.6:21

Maya vol.1:46; vol.4:36, 46; vol.6:22; vol.8:7; *see also* Aztecs, Hieroglyphics, Incas, Pyramid

Measurement vol.6:23; *see also* Calendar, Numbers, Time

Mecca vol. 5:24; vol. 8:27

Medicine vol.3:27; vol.5:45

Mediterranean Sea vol.3:48; vol.4:34

Mercury vol.7:37; vol.9:9

Metal vol.6:24; *see also* Magnet, Meteor, Rocks

Metamorphosis vol. 1:14; vol.6:25; *see also* Amphibian, Insect, Life Cycle

Meteor vol.6:26; *see also* Earth, Solar System

Meteorite vol.6:26

Meter vol. 7:41

Metric system vol.6:23

Mexico vol.6:27; vol.7:7; Index:4; *see also* Aztecs, Maya, North America

Microchip vol.2:46

Middle Ages vol.2:28; vol.5:38; vol.6:28; *see also* Castle, Cathedral, Knight

Middle East vol.5:24,26,33,46; vol.5:46, vol.8:27; vol.10:13

Migration vol. 4:32; vol.6:29; vol.8:38; *see also* Animals

Milne, A.A. vol.7:41

Mineral vol.6:30; vol.8:21

Mining vol.6:30; vol.9:12; vol.10:16; *see also* Metal, Rocks

Mississippi Delta vol.3:17

Mohammed vol. 5:24

Mollusk vol.6:31; vol.8:33; *see also* Animals, Invertebrate

Money vol.6:32

Mongols vol.2:36

Monitor Lizard vol.6:11

Monkey vol.1:15, 20, 25; vol. 6:33; *see also* Ape, Mammal

Monsoon vol.1:35; vol.7:33

Montenegro vol.10:45

Monteverdi, Claudio vol.7:18

Moon vol.6:26, 34; vol.9:9, 16; Index:16; *see also* Earth, Solar System, Space Exploration, Sun

Moose vol.6:35; *see also* Arctic, Deer

Morocco vol.6:36; *see also* Africa, Desert

Moscow vol.8:25

Mosquito vol.4:18; vol.6:37; *see also* Fly, Insect

Moss vol.6:38; *see also* Plants

Moth vol.6:39; *see also* Butterfly, Caterpillar, Insect, Metamorphosis

Mother Teresa vol.1:10

Motor Racing vol.4:13

Motorcycle vol.6:40; *see also* Bicycle, Transportation

Mount Ararat vol. 10:13

Mount Everest vol.6:47

Mountain vol.6:41; *see also* Island, Volcano, and entries for individual countries

Mouse vol.6:42; *see also* Mammal

Movement vol.3:44

Mozart, Wolfgang Amadeus vol.1:28; vol.7:16

Mummy vol.8:7

Muscle vol.5:8; vol.8:45

Mushroom vol.4:27

Music vol.4:19; vol.6:43; *see also* Classical Music, Jazz, Musical Instruments, Percussion Instruments, String Instruments, Wind Instruments

Musical Instruments vol.2:31; vol.4:19; vol.6:44; vol.7:18; vol.9:11; *see also* Music, Percussion Instruments, String Instruments, Wind Instruments

Muslims *see* Islam

Myth vol.6:45; *see also* Legend, Literature, Story

N

Native Americans vol.2:23; vol.3:14; vol.6:45, 46; vol.7:5, 7, 25; vol.10:20; Index:4, 6, 12; *see also* Bison, North America, South America

Nectar vol.1:43; vol.2:16; vol.4:10; vol.5:9; vol.6:37

Nepal vol.6:47; *see also* Asia, Mountain

Neptune vol.7:37; vol.9:9

Netherlands vol.6:48; *see also* Europe

New York vol.5:4; vol.7:46; Index:8, 12

New Zealand vol.1:27; vol.7:4; vol.8:41; *see also* Australia and Oceania, Kiwi

Niagara Falls vol.7:7

Nicaragua vol.7:5; *see also* North America

Nigeria vol.7:6; *see also* Africa

Nile River vol. 3:17, 37, 38; vol. 4:16; vol. 10:16

Noah's Ark vol. 10:13

Noise pollution vol.7:43

Nomad vol.5:4, 20, 33; vol.9:10, 30

North America vol.2:47; vol.7:7; *see also* Continent, Native Americans

North Korea vol.7:8; *see also* Asia, South Korea

North Pole vol.1:22; vol.6:16

Northern Ireland vol.7:9; *see also* Europe, United Kingdom

Norway vol.7:10; *see also* Arctic, Europe, Vikings

Nose vol.9:5

Nuclear Power vol.3:40

Numbers vol.7:11; *see also* Computer, Money

Nutrition vol.7:12; *see also* Food Chain, Human Body

O

Ocean vol.7:13; *see also* Water

Oceania *see* Australia and Oceania

Octopus vol.6:31; vol.7:14; vol. 8:33; *see also* Mollusk, Squid

Oil vol.4:26; vol.5:20, 21, 40; vol.6:4, 30; vol.7:6, 10, 39, 43; vol.8:27

Oil refinery vol.4:26

Olympic Games vol.2:23; vol.4:13; vol.7:15; vol.9:14; *see also* Greece, Ancient

Omnivore vol.1:15; vol.4:20

Opera vol.2:38; vol.7:16; *see also* Drama, Music, Orchestra, Theater

Opossum vol.6:20; vol.7:17; *see also* Mammal, Marsupial

Optical fiber vol.2:45

Orangutan vol.1:20

Orbit vol.2:44; vol.6:34; vol.9:9

Orchestra vol. 2:38; vol.7:16, 18; *see also* Classical Music, Musical Instruments

Ore vol.6:24

Ornithologist vol.1:48

Ostrich vol.3:36; vol.7:19; *see also* Africa, Bird

Otter vol.7:20; *see also* Mammal

Owl vol.3:15; vol.4:4; vol.7:21; *see also* Bird

Oxygen vol.1:8; vol.2:5; vol.4:21; vol.6:12; vol.7:22, 34, 38; vol.8:33; *see also* Air, Lung, Plants

Oyster vol.6:31

P

Pacific Ocean vol.7:7, 13, 25; vol.9:13

Painting vol.7:23; *see also* Art

Pakistan vol.7:24; *see also* Asia

Palestine vol.5:26

Pampas vol.1:23; vol.9:13

Panama vol.7:25; *see also* North America, Waterway

Panama Canal vol.7:25; vol.10:33

Panda vol.7:26; *see also* Endangered Species, Mammal

Papua New Guinea vol.1:27; vol.7:23, 27; *see also* Australia and Oceania

Parasite vol.3:11; vol.4:15; vol.6:5

Parrot vol.7:28; *see also* Bird

Parthenon vol.4:35

Pearl Harbor Index:15

Peary, Robert vol.1:22

Peat vol.4:26; vol.6:38

Penguin vol.7:29; *see also* Antarctica, Bird

Penicillin vol.4:27

Peninsula vol.7:30; *see also* Coast

Percussion Instruments vol.7:31; *see also* Music, Musical Instruments, Orchestra

Persia *see* Iran

Persian Gulf vol.5:40

Peru vol.5:13; vol.7:32; *see also* Incas, South America

Pharaoh vol.3:38; vol.8:7

Philippines vol.7:33; *see also* Asia

Photosynthesis vol.7:34; *see also* Leaf, Plants

Piano vol.7:31

Picasso, Pablo vol.9:17

Pig vol.7:35; *see also* Mammal

Pigeon vol.7:36; *see also* Bird

Piranha vol.4:12

Pitcher Plant vol.3:43

Planets vol.6:34; vol.7:37; vol.9:9; *see also* Solar System, Sun

Plankton vol.4:11; vol.5:32; vol.6:31; vol.8:15, 33, 40

Plantain vol. 3:4

Plants vol.3:43; vol.4:20, 22; vol.5:45; vol.6:6; vol.7:22, 38; vol.8:24, 39; vol.9:8, 25; *see also* Endangered Species, Life Cycle, Photosynthesis

Plastic vol.7:39; *see also* Heat

Platypus vol.6:18; vol.7:40; *see also* Australia, Mammal

Pluto vol.7:37; vol.9:9

Poetry vol.7:41; *see also* Literature

Poland vol.7:42; *see also* Europe

Polar Bear vol.1:22; vol.6:18

Police vol.3:46

Pollen vol.1:43; vol.4:17; vol.6:6

Pollution vol.1:8; vol.3:45; vol.6:12; vol.7:13, 43; vol.8:22

Polyp vol.2:48; vol.5:32

Pop music vol.3:14; vol.7:44; *see also* Music, Musical Instruments

Population *see* entries for individual continents and countries

Porcupine vol.7:45; *see also* Mammal

Port vol.7:46; *see also* Bay, Coast, Ship

Portugal vol.7:47; *see also* Europe

Power Station vol.3:40, 44; vol.6:41

Praying Mantis vol.7:48; *see also* Insect, Invertebrate

Providence, Rhode Island Index:6

Pteranodon vol.8:4

Pterodactyl vol.8:4

Pterosaur vol.8:4; *see also* Dinosaur, Fossil

Puerto Rico vol.8:5; *see also* North America, United States of America

Puffin vol.8:36

Pulley vol.6:14

Punch and Judy vol.8:6

Puppetry vol.8:6; *see also* Drama, Theater

Pygmy vol.3:18; vol.8:26

Pyramid vol.3:37, 38; vol.6:22; vol.8:7; *see also* Egypt; Egypt, Ancient; Maya

Pythagoras vol.6:43

Q

Quéchua Native Americans vol. 3:34; vol.7:32

R

Rabbit vol. 3:30; vol.8:8; *see also* Hare, Mammal

Raccoon vol.8:9; *see also* Mammal

Radio vol.2:45; vol.8:10; *see also* Communication, Television

Railroad vol.8:11; Index:12; *see also* Train, Transportation

Rain *see* Water Cycle, Weather

Rainbow vol.8:12; *see also* Color, Light

Rain Forest vol.2:10; vol.4:21, 36; vol.5:15; vol.6:15, 17; vol.7:5, 6, 7, 25; vol.8:13, 38; vol.10:24; *see also* Forest, Plants

Ramp vol.6:14

Rat vol.8:14; *see also* Mammal

Ray vol.8:15; *see also* Fish, Sea Life

Recycling vol.7:39

Reflection vol. 6:7

Refraction vol.6:7

Reggae Music vol.5:29

Reindeer vol.1:22; vol.4:9

Rembrandt vol.6:48

Renaissance vol.6:28

Reptile vol.3:36; vol.4:45; vol. 6:6; vol.8:16; *see also* Animals

Reservoir vol.5:42; vol.6:41; vol.10:31

Respiratory system vol.5:8; vol.6:12

Revolutionary War Index:8

Rhinoceros vol.3:43; vol.8:17; *see also* Mammal

Rhythm vol.3:14; vol. 6:44; vol.7:41, 44

Rice vol.2:35; vol.3:10, 18, 39; vol.4:7

Rift Valley vol. 5:36

River vol.8:18; *see also* Delta, Flood, Valley, and entries for individual countries

Road vol.8:19; *see also* Transportation

Robot vol.8:20; vol.9:15; *see also* Computer, Laser, Space Exploration

Rock and Roll vol.7:44

Rocks vol.8:21; *see also* Metal, Mining

Rocky Mountains vol.7:7; vol.10:20

Roman Catholicism vol. 5:27; vol. 6:28; vol. 7:32; vol.8:5

Roman Empire vol.3:38; vol.4:35; vol.6:28; vol.8:23

Romania vol.8:22; *see also* Europe

Rome, Ancient vol.6:45; vol.8:19, 23, 30; *see also* Italy, Road

Root vol.8:24, 39; *see also* Plants

Rose Oil vol. 2:14

Rotterdam vol. 7:46

Rubber vol.2:10; vol.6:17; vol.7:38; vol. 10:7

Ruby vol. 6:30

Russia vol.7:18; vol.8:25; *see also* Asia, Europe

Rwanda vol.8:26; *see also* Africa

S

Saga vol. 10:25

Sahara Desert vol.1:7, 11; vol.3:20

St. Patrick vol.5:22

Salmon vol.6:29

Salt vol.6:30

San Francisco vol.1:40; vol.2:24

Satellite vol.2:45; vol.8:10; vol.9:15, 16, 38, 39

Saturn vol.6:34; vol.7:37; vol.9:9

Saudi Arabia vol.8:27; *see also* Asia

Savanna vol.1:7

School of the Air vol.1:26

Scorpion vol.8:28; *see also* Invertebrate

Scotland vol.8:29; *see also* Europe, United Kingdom

Screw vol.6:14

Sculpture vol.1:24; vol.8:30; *see also* Art

Sea Anemone vol.8:31; *see also* Sea Life

Sea Horse vol.8:32; *see also* Fish

Sea Life vol.8:33; *see also* Coral, Fish

Sea Lion vol.8:34; *see also* Mammal, Sea Life

Sea Pollution vol.7:13, 43

Sea Urchin vol.8:35; *see also* Sea Life

Seabird vol.8:36; *see also* Bird, Gull

Seal vol.8:37; *see also* Mammal, Sea Lion

Seasons vol.2:39; vol.8:38; *see also* Climate, Weather

Seaweed vol.7:20; vol.8:33

Seed vol.4:17; vol.6:6; vol.7:38; vol.8:39; *see also* Crop, Plants

Semaphore vol.4:13

Sequoia vol.10:7

Serbia vol.10:45

Shadow vol.6:7

Shakespeare, William vol.3:26

Shark vol.8:40; vol.10:23; *see also* Fish

Sharp, Cecil vol.4:19

Sheep vol.8:41; *see also* Mammal

Ship vol.7:46; vol.8:42; *see also* Barge, Port, Transportation, Waterway

Shofar vol.10:36

Shooting Star *see* Meteor

Shrimp vol.3:11; vol.4:14; vol.8:33

Sign language vol.5:43

Sikhism vol.5:14; vol.8:43

Silk vol.2:36; vol.9:14

Silver vol.6:30

Singapore vol.8:44; *see also* Asia, Port

Skeleton vol.8:45; vol.10:23; *see also* Human Body, Vertebrate

Skunk vol.8:46; *see also* Mammal

Slate vol. 8:21

Slavery Index:5, 9, 11

Sleeping Sickness vol. 4:18

Slovakia vol.8:47; *see also* Europe, Czech Republic

Slovenia vol.8:48; *see also* Yugoslavia

Slug vol.5:19; vol.6:31; vol.9:4; *see also* Mollusk, Snail

Smell vol.9:5, 37; *see also* Taste, Touch

Snail vol.5:19; vol.6:31; vol.9:6; *see also* Mollusk, Slug

Snake vol.4:45; vol.8:16; vol.9:7; *see also* Reptile

Snow vol.10:34

Soccer vol. 3:48

Soil vol.9:8; *see also* Crop, Farming

Solar Power vol.3:40

Solar System vol.9:9, 31; *see also* Planets, Star, Sun

Solid vol.6:21

Solomon Islands vol.1:27

Somalia vol.9:10; *see also* Africa

Sound vol.3:30, 44; vol.9:11; *see also* Ear

South Africa vol.9:12; *see also* Africa

South America vol.2:47; vol.9:13 *see also* Continent

South Korea vol.7:8; vol.9:14; *see also* Asia, North Korea

South Pole vol.1:17; vol.6:16

Soviet Union vol.8:25; *see also* Russia

Space Exploration vol.7:37; vol.8:20; vol.9:15; Index:16; *see also* Moon, Planets, Spacecraft

Spacecraft vol.9:16; *see also* Moon, Space Exploration

Spain vol.9:17; *see also* Europe

Spider vol.9:18; *see also* Invertebrate

Spinning and weaving vol.5:16

Spore vol.4:8, 27; vol.6:38; vol.7:38

Spring vol.8:38

Sputnik I vol.9:15

Squid vol.6:31; vol.9:19; *see also* Mollusk

Squirrel vol.4:45; vol.9:20; *see also* Mammal

Sri Lanka vol.9:21

Stag beetle vol.1:44

Star vol.9:22; *see also* Solar System, Sun

Starfish vol.9:23; *see also* Invertebrate, Sea Life

Statue vol.8:30

Steam engine vol.10:5

Steel vol.5:23; vol.6:16, 24; Index:13

Stegosaurus vol.9:24; *see also* Dinosaur, Fossil

Stem vol.9:25; *see also* Plants

Stilt house vol.1:35, 46; vol.5:5, 15; vol.7:27

Stingray vol.8:15

Stockholm vol.9:33

Stomach vol.5:8

Stone Age vol.9:26; *see also* Bronze Age, Iron Age

Story vol.9:27; *see also* Fable, Fairy Tale, Legend, Literature, Myth

Stream vol.8:18

Stringed Instruments vol.9:28; *see also* Music, Musical Instruments, Orchestra

Submarine vol.9:29; *see also* Ship, Transportation

Submersible vol.9:29

Sudan vol.9:30; *see also* Africa

Suez Canal vol.3:37

Sugar Cane vol.1:37, 46; vol.3:12, 24; vol.4:38

Summer vol.8:38

Sun vol.6:7; vol.7:37; vol.9:9, 22, 31; *see also* Solar System, Star

Sunflower vol.4:17; vol.10:17

Swallow vol.6:29

Swan vol.8:36; vol.9:32; *see also* Bird

Sweden vol.9:33; *see also* Europe

Switzerland vol.9:34; *see also* Europe

Syria vol.9:35; *see also* Asia

Tadpole vol.1:14; vol.4:25; vol.9:45

Taiwan vol.9:36; *see also* Asia, China

Tanker vol.8:42

Tartan vol. 8:29

Tasmania vol. 1:27

Taste vol.9:37; *see also* Smell, Touch

Telephone vol.2:45; vol.9:38; *see also* Communication

Telescope vol.9:15

Television vol.2:21, 43, 45; vol.8:10; vol.9:39; *see also* Communication, Radio

Termite vol.1:4, 18; vol.9:40; *see also* Insect

Tern vol.8:36

Terra Cotta Army vol.2:36

Terrapin vol.10:14

Thailand vol.9:41; *see also* Asia

Thames Barrier vol.4:16

Theater vol.9:42; *see also* Drama, Opera

Thunder vol.6:8; vol.9:11; vol.10:34

Tidal wave vol.3:32

Tiger vol.1:25; vol.9:43; *see also* Mammal

Time vol.9:44; *see also* Calendar, Measurement, Seasons

Time zone vol.9:44

Toad vol.4:45; vol.9:45; *see also* Amphibian, Frog, Metamorphosis

Toadstool vol.4:27

Tobacco vol.3:12, 19

Tobago *see* Trinidad and Tobago

Tongue vol.9:37

Tools vol.2:11; vol.5:23; vol.9:26

Tooth vol.9:46; *see also* Human Body

Torah vol.5:34

Tornado vol.9:47; vol.10:34; *see also* Hurricane, Weather

Tortoise vol.8:16; vol.9:48; *see also* Reptile, Turtle

Touch vol.10:4; *see also* Smell, Taste

Train vol.10:5; *see also* Railroad, Transportation

Transportation vol. 10:6; *see also* Railroad, Road, Waterway

Transylvania vol.8:22

Travois vol.6:46

Tree vol.1:8; vol.8:38; vol.10:7; *see also* Forest, Rainforest, Wood

Tributary vol.8:18

Triceratops vol.10:8, 23; *see also* Dinosaur, Fossil

Trinidad and Tobago vol.10:9; *see also* South America

Truck vol.10:10; *see also* Road, Transportation

Trumpet vol.6:43

Tuatara vol.8:16

Tugboat vol.1:38; vol.8:42

Tundra vol.1:22; vol.10:11; *see also* Arctic

Tunisia vol.10:12; *see also* Africa

Turkey (country) vol.10:13; *see also* Asia, Europe

Turnpike vol.8:19

Turtle vol.3:36; vol.8:16; vol.10:14; *see also* Reptile, Tortoise

Tutsi vol.8:26

Typhoon vol.5:11

Tyrannosaurus vol.3:21; vol.10:8, 15; *see also* Dinosaur, Fossil

U

Uganda vol.10:16; *see also* Africa

Ukraine vol.10:17; *see also* Europe

Ultrasound vol.9:11

U.N. Security Council vol. 10:19

United Kingdom (U.K.) vol.10:18; *see also* Europe

United Nations (U.N.) vol.4:13; vol.5:21; vol.10:19

United States of America (U.S.A.) vol.10:20; Index:8-16; *see also* American History, Native Americans, North America

Ural Mountains vol.3:48; vol.8:25

Uranus vol.7:37; vol.9:

V

Valley vol.10:21; *see also* Mountain, River

Valley of the Kings vol.3:38

Van Gogh, Vincent vol.1:24; vol.6:48

Vatican City vol.5:27

Venezuela vol.10:22; *see also* South America

Venus vol.7:37; vol.9:9

Vertebrate vol.10:23; *see also* Invertebrate, Skeleton

Vermeer vol.6:48

Vibration vol.9:11

Vietnam vol.10:24; *see also* Asia

Vikings vol.6:45; vol.7:10; vol.10:25; *see also* Denmark, Norway, Sweden

Violin vol.9:28

Virus vol.10:26; *see also* Bacteria

Volcano vol.1:23, 27; vol.3:4, 31; vol.4:36; vol.5:12, 15, 25, 27, 30; vol.6:41; vol.7:4, 5, 13, 32; vol.10:27; *see also* Mountain

Vowel vol.1:13

Vulture vol.10:28; *see also* Bird

W

Wagner, Richard vol.7:16

Wales vol.10:29; *see also* Europe, United Kingdom

Washington, George Index:8

Wasp vol.10:30; *see also* Bee, Insect

Water vol.10:31; *see also* Water Cycle

Water Cycle vol.10:32; *see also* Water

Water Pollution vol.7:43

Water Power vol.3:40

Waterway vol.10:33; *see also* Barge, Ship, Transportation

Weapons vol.2:11; vol.5:23, 38; vol.9:26

Weather vol.2:39; vol.3:31; vol.8:38; vol.10:34; *see also* Climate

Wedge vol.6:14

Whale vol.10:23, 35; *see also* Dolphin, Mammal

Wheel vol.6:14

Wildebeest vol.4:20

Wind Instruments vol.10:36; *see also* Music, Musical Instruments, Orchestra

Winter vol.8:38

Wolf vol.1:25; vol.3:22; vol.10:37; *see also* Dog, Mammal

Wolverine vol.10:38; *see also* Mammal

Wood vol.10:7, 39; *see also* Forest, Rain Forest, Tree

Woodlouse vol.3:11; vol.10:40; *see also* Crustacean, Invertebrate

Woodpecker vol.10:41; *see also* Bird

World War One vol.10:42; Index:13; *see also* World War Two

World War Two vol.5:34; vol.10:43; Index:15; *see also* World War One

World Wide Web vol.5:18

Worm vol.5:19; vol.9:8; vol.10:44; *see also* Invertebrate

Wright Brothers vol.1:9; Index:13

Y

Year vol.2:18

Yugoslavia vol.10:45; *see also* Europe

Z

Zaire *see* Democratic Republic of Congo (DRC)

Zambia vol.10:46; *see also* Africa

Zebra vol.10:47; *see also* Horse, Mammal

Zimbabwe vol.10:48; *see also* Africa

Zoologist vol.1:15